BEHIND THE SCENES
BASKETBALL

by James Monson

Lerner Publications ◆ Minneapolis

Lerner Publications Company
A division of Lerner Publishing Group, Inc.
241 First Avenue North
Minneapolis, MN 55401 USA

For reading levels and more information, look up this title at www.lernerbooks.com.

The images in this book are used with the permission of: © Thearon W. Henderson/Getty Images Sport/Getty Images, p. 1; © Gregory Shamus/Getty Images Sport/Getty Images, pp. 4–5; © Jason Miller/Getty Images Sport/Getty Images, p. 6; © Monkey Business Images/Shutterstock.com, pp. 8–9; © Jayne Kamin-Oncea/Getty Images Sport/Getty Images, p. 10; © Michael Reaves/Getty Images Sport/Getty Images, pp. 12–13; © Matteo Marchi/Getty Images Sport/Getty Images, p. 14; © Maddie Meyer/Getty Images Sport/Getty Images, p. 17; © Zhong Zhi/Getty Images Sport/Getty Images, pp. 18–19; © Williams Paul/Icon Sportswire/Getty Images, pp. 20–21; © Ronald Cortes/Getty Images Sport/Getty Images, p. 23; © Emma McIntyre/Caruso Affiliated/Getty Images Entertainment/Getty Images, pp. 24–25; © Allen Berezovsky/Getty Images Entertainment/Getty Images, pp. 26–27; © wavebreakmedia/Shutterstock.com, p. 29.

Front cover: © Thearon W. Henderson/Getty Images Sport/Getty Images.

Main body text set in Myriad Pro.
Typeface provided by Adobe.

Library of Congress Cataloging-in-Publication Data

Names: Monson, James, 1994– author.
Title: Behind the scenes basketball / James Monson.
Description: Minneapolis : Lerner Publications, [2020] | Series: Inside the sport | Includes bibliographical references and index. | Audience: Ages: 7–11. | Audience: Grades: 4–6.
Identifiers: LCCN 2018049356 (print) | LCCN 2019003035 (ebook) | ISBN 9781541556270 (eb pdf) | ISBN 9781541556096 (lb : alk. paper) | ISBN 9781541574359 (pb : alk. paper)
Subjects: LCSH: Basketball—United States—Juvenile literature. | Basketball players—United States—Juvenile literature. | Basketball players—United States—Conduct of life—Juvenile literature.
Classification: LCC GV885.1 (ebook) | LCC GV885.1 .M667 2019 (print) | DDC 796.323—dc23

LC record available at https://lccn.loc.gov/2018049356

Manufactured in the United States of America
1-CG-7/15/19

CONTENTS

GETTING TO
THE TOP

With just seconds left in the game, Stephen Curry of the Golden State Warriors stood with a smile on his face. Those few seconds were all that separated him from the 2018 National Basketball Association (NBA) championship. Curry and his teammates had played through a tiring season and three rounds of playoffs. That led them to the NBA Finals, where they faced superstar LeBron James and the Cleveland Cavaliers. The Warriors had won the first three games of the best-of-seven series. Now they just needed to win this game to become champions. It would be their third championship in four years.

Stephen Curry makes a move during Game 4 of the 2018 NBA Finals against the Cleveland Cavaliers. ▶

FACTS
at a Glance

- Some men's basketball players have gone straight to the NBA at eighteen years old. But starting in 2006, players had to be at least one year out of high school before entering the NBA Draft.

- Many players in the Women's National Basketball Association (WNBA) also play on professional basketball teams overseas during the off-season.

- Many NBA and WNBA players do charity work or attend events where they can meet their fans.

Stephen Curry and Kevin Durant hug after Game 4 ▶ of the 2018 NBA Finals.

In that final game, Curry commanded the court. He hit long three-point shots. He knocked down short jump shots. He also helped his team play good defense. With the Warriors winning in a blowout, Curry headed to the bench for the final time that season. He watched the last few seconds knowing his team was about to win the championship. When the clock hit zero, Curry and his teammates rushed to center court. They celebrated with a group hug.

The Warriors played hard for their championship win. But professional basketball players do a lot more work than what fans see on the court. There are many hours of preparation and training done behind the scenes. When players make the right moves on and off the court, they could end up winning championships like Curry.

CHAPTER 1

MAKING THE JUMP

Most professional basketball players started playing the sport when they were kids. Young basketball players can join teams organized through their schools or communities. Serious players work hard on their high school teams.

Most kids who want to play in college or professionally play on American Athletic Union (AAU) teams. These teams are in almost every community. AAU teams play in the summer when school teams aren't playing. Some of the teams travel long distances for games and tournaments. College coaches often attend AAU tournaments to recruit players.

High school basketball teams are important for kids who want to grow up to play in the NBA or WNBA. ▶

Los Angeles Lakers president of basketball operations Magic Johnson (left) introduces one of the team's 2018 draft picks, Moritz Wagner, at a press conference.

Men's basketball players must be a year out of high school before entering the NBA Draft. Most play a year of college basketball in the United States. But some leave the country for a year to play in professional leagues. Heading overseas is becoming more popular because players get paid to play in European and Asian leagues but not to play college basketball. Starting in 2019, some top eighteen-year-olds are also invited to play professionally in the NBA's G League. This is a minor league where players can work on their skills while waiting for their shot at NBA glory.

Players sign contracts when they are drafted to the NBA. The players selected among the top ten or fifteen picks usually play with NBA teams as rookies. Other first-year players play in the NBA's G League.

Women's players must be at least twenty-two years old to play in the WNBA. Many play four years of college basketball. Then they hope to be selected in the WNBA Draft and play professionally. However, the WNBA doesn't pay as well as the NBA. Because of this, many women's players also play professionally overseas in the off-season.

GETTING READY FOR GAME DAY

Basketball players start their mornings by eating a healthful breakfast. Some players like to eat heavy food like waffles. Others might have an egg-white omelet. Most basketball players eat breakfast around 8:00 or 9:00 a.m. when they have a game that night.

After breakfast, it's time to head to the arena. Most teams do a morning shootaround to get warmed up for that night's game. This practice usually lasts an hour. It's a good time for players to work on skills such as shooting and rebounding. There is also time for the team to work together on different plays.

Atlanta Hawks players practice in a shootaround. ▶

Russell Westbrook of the Oklahoma City Thunder warms up
before a game.

Players usually talk to media reporters after morning
practice. These are short interviews that take place on the court
after the practice. Players then head back to the locker room for
a snack.

Many players nap before games. This happens in the early afternoon at the players' homes or at their hotel if the team is playing a road game. At about 4:00 p.m., most players eat something light, like a sandwich. Then they head back to the arena for that night's game.

Players arrive ready to warm up for the game. They'll practice more shooting and stretch their bodies with a trainer. Players also try to get ready for the game mentally. Many listen to music or meditate.

The coach usually comes into the locker room right before the game to discuss strategy with the team. Players head onto the court minutes before the opening tipoff to be introduced in front of the fans.

Stats Spotlight
2.55

That's the number of miles an NBA player runs up and down the court during a game. New technology allows teams to track how far their players are running in games. Teams can then use this information to make sure players are using their energy in the best way possible. Jimmy Butler averaged the most of any NBA player when he ran about 2.66 miles per game in the 2015–16 season while playing for the Chicago Bulls.

NBA and WNBA games can be tiring. Players try to conserve their energy so they can still play well in the last few minutes of a close game. That's often when teams play tight defense to try to prevent the opponent from scoring. They also work hard to get a good shot on offense.

After the game, big-name players might have a press conference. However, most of the players are interviewed in front of their lockers. Sometimes players can get frustrated with the criticism they get from the media. Other times, though, these interviews can be fun. Players might wear funny outfits. Russell Westbrook of the Oklahoma City Thunder once wore a bathrobe and sweatpants. Stephen Curry has brought his daughter to press conferences.

Players eat a full dinner after the game. Then it's off to bed. They usually have a couple of days to recover before the next game.

Al Horford of the Boston Celtics speaks at a press conference. ▶

CHAPTER 3

STAYING IN SHAPE

Professional basketball players need to stay healthy and continue improving their skills. Players practice a lot on days when they don't have games. They work on skills like shooting or rebounding. Players head to team practice courts at all hours of the day to work on their shots. Zach LaVine of the Chicago Bulls sometimes practices shooting late at night.

Teammates also practice together. They work on different plays. There are also times when the team watches videos from their previous games or from an upcoming opponent's games to strategize and improve.

Joel Embiid of the Philadelphia 76ers practices between games. ▶

During the off-season, players still practice their on-court skills. But they also focus on getting stronger in the weight room. Many players have personal trainers they work with in the off-season.

Women's players often spend the WNBA off-season playing in professional leagues in other countries, such as Russia or China. This is because WNBA players get paid much less than NBA players. They can make money playing in other leagues during the off-season.

▲

Jasmine Thomas of the Connecticut Sun stretches before a game.

Basketball players can be at risk for injuries because they play so many games. They don't wear as much protective equipment as football or hockey players. But some do wear padding under their shorts or jerseys. These are made so players don't feel it as much if they get hit hard while playing.

Teams want their players to be safe. They also want each player to be successful. Technology has changed how teams help players do this. For example, ShotTracker technology can tell teams instantly how well a player is shooting the ball from different parts of the court. Teams then use this information to move players around so they're in the best position to succeed.

Rajon Rondo of the
◀ Los Angeles Lakers works
hard during practice.

CHAPTER 4

MAKING AN IMPACT

The off-season is a perfect time for NBA and WNBA players to connect with their communities. One easy way for players to do this is through charity work. Most teams organize charity events. Their players might read to children, visit sick people in hospitals, or donate clothes to people in need.

Many players also do charity work on their own. Tina Charles of the New York Liberty has worked with groups that focus on heart health. She donated three years of her WNBA salary to charities that help work toward preventing heart attacks.

Chris Paul of the Los Angeles Clippers reads to a child during a holiday charity event. ▶

Outside of charity work, many players spend their off-season traveling or visiting with family. They might attend events like the ESPYs or the NBA Awards show. Many players stay connected with their fans through Twitter or Instagram. These social media websites help fans see what players are like off the court.

NBA players are famous all over the world. More people are playing basketball worldwide. And new technology is helping players perfect their skills. It seems basketball will continue to be a popular sport for years to come.

◄ **James Harden of the Houston Rockets poses for a photo with his mom at the NBA Awards show after he won the Most Valuable Player Award in 2018.**

YOUR TURN

NBA players like Stephen Curry and Kevin Durant know how to make baskets in big games. Here's one way young players can practice making a shot under pressure with some friends.

First, find a group of at least four people. The more people, the more fun it is! Then, get everyone lined up single file behind the free-throw line. Everyone should be in one long line. Make sure there is just one basketball used for this drill.

The person who is first in line shoots a free throw. Then she passes the ball to the next person. Here's where it gets fun. As soon as someone makes a shot, the pressure is on. The next person has to make his shot. If he does not, he is out of the game. Once someone misses a shot, the pressure is off. The remaining players continue until another shot is made.

This drill goes until there is just one person left. It's a good way to work on shooting the ball with a little pressure.

Young basketball players can practice together with a shooting drill.

Practicing drills like this one helps players feel more comfortable on the court during an actual game.

GLOSSARY

blowout
when one team beats the other team by a lot of points

charity
related to an organization that helps other people or raises money for a good cause

contracts
agreements between a player and a team that tells each side how many years a player will play for the team and how much money he will make

criticism
negative or disapproving comments

cryotherapy
a way to use low temperatures to relieve stress in muscles

ESPYs
a famous awards show presented by ESPN, a sports TV network

glory
praise for a great achievement

meditate
to clear one's mind as a form of relaxing

overseas
in a country that one has to travel across an ocean to get to

press conference
an event at which athletes or other people answer questions from many media reporters at once

salary
the amount of money someone makes per year at her job

trainer
a professional that helps someone improve their physical fitness

FURTHER
INFORMATION

Bryant, Howard. *Legends: The Best Players, Games, and Teams in Basketball.*
　　New York: Philomel Books, 2017.

Junior NBA
https://jr.nba.com

Levit, Joe. *Basketball's G.O.A.T.: Michael Jordan, LeBron James, and More.*
　　Minneapolis: Lerner Publications, 2020.

Naismith Memorial Basketball Hall of Fame
http://hoophall.com

National Basketball Association
http://www.nba.com

Savage, Jeff. *Basketball Super Stats.* Minneapolis: Lerner Publications, 2018.

INDEX

ABOUT THE AUTHOR

James Monson is a sportswriter based in the Minneapolis-Saint Paul area. He has written articles that have appeared in various publications across the country. He has a degree in print/digital sports journalism.